My Last Name is Volcano

A Quotumentary

Leah & Isaac Wedaman

Edited by David G. Wedaman, Ph.D.

Least Shining Crescent Press

Least Shining Crescent Press

Cambridge, Massachusetts, USA

www.leastshiningcrescent.com

ISBN 978-0-578-02891-0

Least Shining Crescent Press publishes unique books expressive of life in all its glory.   Consult our website (www.leastshiningcrescent.com) for more information.

For inquiries or whatever contact us by email:

leastshiningcrescent@gmail.com.

Editor's Prologue

Reader, you have the distinct pleasure to be poised on the threshold of a unique experience. In your hands is a strange product that has been called sometimes a "quotumentary," sometimes a "micro-epistolary," and sometimes a "novel in quotes." Whichever, it's much more than a slice of fluid life, captured and crystallized in the 300 or so pithy and eloquent vitamins of journalism produced by Leah and Isaac Wedaman between December, 2008 and June, 2009. But it is much less than *Clarissa*. More than *Gone with the Wind* but rather less than a short story by Guy de Maupassant. Like butter, but not at all like cream, etc.

I would love to say more about how much *My Last Name is Volcano* has influenced those in the writers' immediate circle, but I abhor the thought of further delaying or otherwise just influencing your own trip to the Volcano's edge. How to describe the experience of anything meaningful, I mean, really? Suffice it to say that those of us who have had the honor have found in the following pages nothing less than the pure and unrefined stuff of hope, dreams, consolation, love, hate, warmth, horror, and perhaps a little bit of confusion. And Volcanic fire. In short just about every human emotion, which is nice. You are about to learn why many people have surely been inclined to feel that *My Last Name is Volcano* might profitably be the only book they would need to take if embarking upon one of those infamous "three-hour tours," that always last so much longer than three hours!

"O, for a muse of fire, that would ascend the brightest heaven of invention?" Here it is! Go forth and edify.

Cambridge, Massachusetts, USA

June 12, 2009

Contents

A long, long, long, long time ago I licked my lips.

I have 29 teeth.

Superman! Get off the computer! OK, don't get off the computer. 'Bye!

How do you spell "trailer?" That's a long word.

There was a princess who got married, and then she goed crazy.

How do you put tires on cars?

Do you have any snacks?

I wish we could eat worm bones.

If I see a wolf, I run fast.

I'm making a rain. I'm making a rain cloud. I'm making the cheeks.

That's so yummy I can eat a door!

I'm making a truck. This is the smokestack coming out. My truck is not a truck, it's a machine.

Everything on Leah is pink!

Need to go to pirate school.

How do you make cheese?

Ah, money.

I can eat a million ducks.

His face was almost to the sky. His arm was longer than Mama's but not as long as yours. His head was bigger than anyone's in the world.

I did the right thing! I read the book and put it back where it was supposed to go!

I ate soap and then I washed it down with water.

I didn't feel my teeth crunching on the chips. I knew I needed to be crunching on the chips, but when I looked Isaac had them.

I care about cars.

If you do something that you need to do, you change to another number.

I grabbed the Tinkertoy box from Leah, and it wasn't an accident, and it was on purpose, and I said I was sorry.

The bad lady can't find us. We're going to sneak inside our house and have a nice fire.

I wanna watch *Knight Rider*. I love *Knight Rider*.

Aunt Sarah says I can't have the chocolate because she's going to give it to herself.

I want the cow.

Every night if the storm blows off a tire then we need to fix it every day.

I want to go to boy dance class.

I didn't almost bit him on the foot.

I'm going upstairs to grab Papa.

I flew away like Mama.

Instead of "the end," I say "D. O."

I had chocolate beads for supper.

My job is to put shine on everything.

I have some bad news for you. Isaac was kicking me on your chair.

My nose isn't doing what I ask it to do.

If I had a left, if I was going to a party, I saw a left.

S ometimes I nudge. I'm just
called the nudger.

Pokey things are danger.

Those are fashion boots for girls.

P ush the button so you can get the beanie. Pop out, Beanie! Pop out!

A long time ago I was an astronaut, and I went in a rocket ship, and I went to space.

Can you put five pinches on my arm? I winned.

Does this show have cars in it?

I want the matching cherry pants!

D on't go too close to that
Nissan.

I wanted to wear a dress under a shirt.

I did go in your ship for one second, so now I'm not gonna do it.

If anyone calls for a tissue, I will give them a tissue from my box. I call it a tissue house. If anyone needs tissues, call out for tissue.

I don't want Papa to drive.

If you make fun of the people who are in our stage, you have to leave our stage.

I love Hamburger Helper.

Smell my hair, it smells like dinner.

I took your baby out of bed.

This spider is walking on two legs.

I want a house with a hammock next to it.

C an we race down there and
come back here? Can we really
do that? Can we?

It tastes like lights.

I'm a bag. A bag with a face.

Mama poked my sister in the eye.

I'm not Leah, I'm Superstar.
Superstar can do anything. When
there's an emergency, Superstar
can skip faster.

My big boy comes here and he drinks a shake, then he goes home and eats his dinner, then he goes to sleep in the daytime! Ha ha ha.

I'm not talking to you, I'm talking to my hand.

We ate pancakes and avocado and sauce, except Leah's was naked. And so was mine.

I'm supposed to be in front. Says who? I said it.

B atman's gonna break that man's gun. 'Cuz he's got protection. *Protection.*

L et's sing "Molly Malone." Papa, can you sing the die part?

Do my eyes look like girl eyes? I want girl eyes.

Little bug, I ate your seatbelt.

He just has a ball of hair. A big ball.

My big girl has a show and it's called *Bonkie on the Heady*, and the monster's name is Jeepie.

I didn't like the octopus, and I didn't like the monsters. The octopus looked like a Cyclops. Cyclopses have one eye.

Dim Sum is coming on the train.

I drinked kid wine and ate cheese.

I'm making a race car that will eat these lines. I'm making a Cyclops. I'm making big balls and little balls.

I have to be a detective.

Papa, I have to tell you something really short, and it's not long. Come on, Binkie, I'm going to give you a splinter, 'bye!

I want to come in your ship. Can I have some chewdigans?

Papa, I'm nice again.

I f you stand in the street and cars are comin' and they drive over you, you will be flat. That's not good.

Papa, the computer is not doing the things I want it to do.

L ook, that cow is eating hay.

Papa, you can touch this because there's no fire and no pointy thing on it.

My big boy doesn't like beans or apples.

S ome heavy things fall down.

Sometimes I have tears. And sometimes I cry.

I never said goodbye with a stick.

Who taped my volcano?

I f anybody wants to come in my ship, it has a lot of food.

All the trucks are going in the garage. Except one truck broke. One truck bumped itself.

That dog sniffed my Muumi's ear.

Egg island? I love Egg Island!

We need to drive slowly because there's a monster up there.

His first name is Motorcycle.
His second name is Octopus.
And his other name is . . .
Smokestack, you got it, Daddy.

The jellyfish is floating in our room. Better get him.

I ate a duck in one gulp.

All of these cars are allergic and there's a monster coming.

I binged a boo.

Everbody needs to come over and say "I don't like you."

I don't like earwax, they don't like me. I have earwax in my nose.

I was coming to help. When they tried to shoot me, I was running.

I never ate haunted jelly.

This is my safety. To keep me safe from a monster. It's my monster thing.

I thought Leah was the sink.

Isaac, I have one more candy for your big boy. It's not dog poop. Do you know what it is?

I wanna climb up a beanstalk to get to the cereal.

I call it a tissue house. If anyone needs tissues, call out for tissue.

I'm drinking hemp milk.

We are not OK because that was a really bad, bad crash.

I'm making a horse truck. Horses drive this truck.

Is I'm drinking hemp milk?

I'm on the edge of anger.

The dentist counts our teeth. I have four teeth.

My big boy found the gum,
and he fell on the sidewalk.
Because it made him fall.

They only have heads. The Little Kids, they don't have legs. And they don't have bellies.

M y head is popping out.
Come on Ed Binkie, we're
going in my house.

Papa, you need to be quiet because we're on the stage and the lights are off. But you can open your eyes. And turn your things off.

Papa, I'm gonna putch you. I'm sorry, I didn't mean it.

No! It's not fair. Isaac said there are no girl dinosaurs. But some are girls.

The ghost car keeps driving everywhere. It keeps pushin' cars and mushin' cars.

But he's fixing it and it's already fixed.

Your Papa drives this van, and when he gets thirsty, he opens the back and has a drink. His cousin sits there.

I will ask you one more time to don't crash into my cousins.

Boys are pineapples, and girls are beets.

Lops are like raindrops, only they have tails and backs like a leaf. Like a monkey only smaller.

Haunted jelly is what ghosts eat.

Papa, you have to bend your head.

I dreamed about trucks and busses. And vans. Pickup Trucks.

When I was trying to draw, a little bit of draw came on me.

I heard my sister cough.

When we were young, we drived on everything we were not supposed to drive on.

I said to Mama, "When Papa comes home, can we watch *Speed Racer*?" and she said, "Yes, you can."

B atboy, I am in trouble. Get the hoy.

I want to sleep in the street and let cars run over me. Because I love them.

Girl eyes can only go up and down, up and down. That's what I said.

It's a guy on a motorcycle. His name's Sardines.

I think I hear a raccoon.

Let's laugh about it, clap about it, and jump about it on the bed.

I will have a little bit of everything and a little bit more of everything.

M

otorcycle Octopus Smokestack is my big boy's name.

If you want some cake, you need to come to my birthday and ask your mom and do things.

My big boy has a show, and it's named *Who's the Biggest Person?* and it's wroten by Juney Backa. That's his name.

Milk tastes bitter when I eat the pudding.

My last name is Dump Truck.

My big girl's birthday she got a chocolate cake and pink frosting. And when it's nighttime, she watchted a show and readed a book with her mom.

My papa sang a song about a girl who died and a nice ghost. She rode a barrow with tacos and mussels.

There's jellyfish under this tunnel, so someone needs to put their foot behind so you can not get out.

One day when Leah and Isaac are big maybe we can see a real caveman.

This is where I mush my candy for my big girl.

The sign says "Go Away."

This car has to get more air into that little hole.

They have two eggs at the Museum of Science in the beehive in case they want bee babies.

This is a fake rock with bad things under it.

Attention, passengers. The next Red Line train to Ashmont is now approaching.

This is how you make an eye. I'm making a hot balloon.

B irds don't grow. They stay
how they are.

We're almost ready. We're going to be right on time. We're just making the birthday cake.

He has 3 smokestacks. That's a lot of smokestacks.

When I was singing "ten-eleven-six at the ladybug picnic," Isaac was hitting me and throwing things at me and bonking me on the head

How long did you beed at work? Five years?

How can they get out? One has a cape and one doesn't.

I don't like beautiful things. I love Spiderman and he loves me. I love monster trucks and motorcycles. You're the one who loves beautiful things.

I am a pirate. I just want to see your money.

I had like five cherries. And like five cars.

This show is called *Konk in the Butt.*

I never get to do anything.

One day I was walking in the street, and it had a boot on it. Goodbye.

I poked them in the hat.

They had a house with a cat on the woods, and the cat is arm lifts up, and that's their door.

I wanna get out of this spooky room.

Some Little Kids are kinda listening and have to go to time out.

I wasn't creakin', I was just peekin'.

We can't put the toys in because the fire is too heavy to lift up the blanket.

I'm making a ghost. These are the legs of it.

When your big boy's sick, he can have some candy and a pick thing. And shake it.

I'm taking the day off.

What about lollipops, if they don't have any cake?

If cars get stuck, this car can drive in mud.

Nobody wants to see us playing with their big boy . . . Nobody wants to see us touching the eggs in their trees . . . Nobody wants to see us sitting on their step . . . Nobody wants to see us going up to their door . . .

If I see that, I will poke it with a fork.

Do martyrs say "Ow" a lot?

Knowledge goes on your hair?

Egg, egg, egg, egg, egg, egg.

Mama said she's too tired to put on my socks.

I see a boy with a pony tail. Papa, one day you were having a shirt on and you were wearing a pony tail without glasses. He has glasses.

One grogger is in the synagogue, and one grogger is out of the synagogue.

Isaac keeps telling me I'm a bad guy, I'm a bad guy, I'm a bad guy. Look how many times he keeps telling me I'm a bad guy.

P apa, I have to crash you. I can crash kids, and I can crash cars, and I can crash buildings . . .

Isaac wiped his nose on my smell!

Papa's feet and my feet feel great!

Isaac, this is like a kooky-looking, kooky-kooky-kooky looking car. It's so kooky-looking.

You can't walk around on no feet.

Isaac, you're breaking my car! Are you fixing it?

Binkie Jones is a good guy, and he lives across the street.

It's just a little wake-up time because I think bad guys.

Can I put salt in my drink?

It's loud. I'm gonna do a not loud.
Is this loud?

Fake things and toys are not heavy.

No! Isaac hit me with that ball right on the neck.

I can eat all the ducks in the world.
I can eat a hundred ducks.

We have to go back up to the raindrops because the mountain is sad.

I have a fire tent.

Chickens don't know to go potty.

I wanna go to the end of the rainbow. I wanna see the golden pot.

I pushed a button. Sorry, sorry, sorry, sorry, sorry.

I'm tired because I yawned.

Leah's bird has a mad eye because he's bad. But a little bit he's good. He has sad inside his body. No, goodness.

M y big boy is sleeping, so we have to be very quiet and watch *Speed Racer*.

Maybe the sun is sick.

My poops are shaped like dolphins.

One computer is with a Papa skoldekick and the book is wroten by Shoes-n Juno.

The rock monster broke and the water splashed away.

When I go in the pool, my mouth goes like this.

When I was a baby, I really loved *Speed Racer*, too.

Chewygons are chewy. They are little gons for kids.

When they want to make avocado and nuts in the back of their car, they just do it.

I love beautiful things. Like Princesses. Ariel's sister is named Aurora.

Have you ever seen a monkey drink coffee?

My last name is Volcano.

How do you drive to Salem?

I made a turkey.

I am not a ghost.

Someone is holding on to a newspaper for a very long time. And it's Isaac. *That* Isaac.

I don't like your name.

The Little Kids are coming in your room to bite you.

I nudge about all the things with wheels.

When I'm twelve, can I eat gum?

I wish I could drive a big truck.

Does our movie stop working if we make a copy? How do we make a copy? Let's not talk about making a copy of the movie.

L eah said some wrong things about Spiderman.

The little mouse got a tissue. She throwed it in the potty.

L eah gave my hand a little bath.

The Little Kids weren't listening to our words, so we put them in jail.

My big boy likes peanut butter.

S ometimes you be mad, Papa.

Cars don't matter, they like danger.

When Mama picked me up at preschool, I didn't scream like a baby, and I didn't flop on the ground like a fish.

How do you make a road?

My pool has no black stuff in it. Look, I made a ghost eye.

I don't need lip jelly. My lips are always lip.

Earwax. Yuck. It smells like numbers.

I had too many baths, Papa. I had too many baths.

The sign says no balls at parties.
You can only dance at parties.

I only like things that have wheels.

That's not vegetable soup. It's lucky water. And it has mermaids in it.

I wanna say . . . uh . . . I love you.

You guys made me do a lot.

I went outside to plant tomato seeds.

You have to stop the podcast.
I am not talking.

Mama put this stamp on me. I got those stamps from what? Where did I get those stamps?

You're not singing! She needs to die.

My six-wheeled car is getting fixed in the fix shop because it has a flat tire.

L olly Pop Golden was with his two friends and they were wroten by a fish named Skocky Doodle. And they were caught in a soap fish's mouth. In the pool where they were swimming there was a big swimming pool, and it was really hot.

That's so good, I can eat a sheep!

Maybe it's rocky, and maybe they're crashing.

My big boy watches *Pink Panther* every day.

My big girl is not full because she hasn't ate anything, so I am going to give her some candy.

L et's go to Target to buy me some Matchbox cars.

Nobody wants to see my naked legs.

This one is getting a big shop. This wheel is bein' cut. This wheel has to be taked off. It has a stink on it. These tires have a stinks on them.

These are the pictures of ghosts trying to scare the "conkas" but they can't scare, they're just balls.

When I was a baby, I loved cars. Every day I loved cars.

Birds grow. Teddy and David are here.

Papa, where is my six-wheeled car?

I don't want you to eat my sandwiches. So you better watch out. You are becoming a monster who eats other people's food.

One of dinosaur's rubs bumped.

We have to go, Papa. The mermaids are coming.

That car is an Audi.

Can I put 20 flags on the window?

We had the crash on the roof so we got Band-Aids on the roof.

I have to shake it because the Little Kids are on there.

When you see a monster, you have to eat him and capture him.

L ittle mouse saw pillows that the dinosaur was here.

Your belly is a dangerous place.
You can't move it.

They do have legs, but they can't walk because they eat all the time.

Only some pants I need.

When I was a baby, I wanted to eat my foot.

When I was a baby, I smoked a pipe.

Where can our house be, if the rain falls on us?

The bees are making pollen on my ear. It feels so hot. I have allergy attack.

Where is France?

This is my wallet, and it's full of money.

I know you're excited about playing *Sorry*, but you have to follow the rules.

When Mama is asleep, can we watch *Speed Racer?*

I'm gonna eat your leg off.

That Honda Pilot parked next to that Audi.

It's something that you ride on, and when you ride it something goes around.

We named our balloon Squeaky.

My big girl dreamed about clowns. And I dreamed about pillows.

When the bug was sleeping, we ate his hair off.

Tar off his feet. Put footprints.
Put footprints.

We learned about butterflies and octopus and caterpillars.

There's a little bit of cats and a little bit of thunder.

You have to count to five before you eat the monster.

They're babies, so they don't have names yet.

What is Heaven's last name?

When I talk to somebody, nobody is listening!

That snake looks like an urban worm.

Everyone likes me because I'm not very bad to them.

When I was two, I fell out of a tree.

Everything in my room is hurting me because nobody is cleaning it up.

The sun is making my cars hot.

I dreamed about car keys.

Pokes are bad. Long pokers are bad.

I was not the one who was fighting over you, you were the one who was fighting over me.

P apa, how do you make a truck?

Papi, look: new soap! It's squishy!

The Little Kids took our books, so I hit them with a bat and put them in the trash.

The cousins are not buried yet.

These cars don't know what to do.

Who's gonna be the bad guy
if we're both good?

When I was a baby, I wanted to eat my baby gum.

Why do you want to rub my head? Because it smells so good?

Why does Ford have its name inside a tire?

You are not a ghost, but it's danger in here.

Then type "who-in." That means computer, I am saying.

Cars don't have a face.

This used to be one of my big boy's favorite highways.

How is it Batboy doesn't do what I say?

Who took my six-wheeled car?

I wish I could dance like that. Maybe I don't wanna dance like that.

Birds can be a boy or a girl.

I yelled too loud, and my toothbrush fell out.

My big boy likes sour.

Maybe the big folks have to let the teachers at dance class learn me how to dance.

That sign says "No Turn On Red."

A lift or a left? Skonkie Fish is my running konkadoodle.

www.ingramcontent.com/pod-product-compliance
Lightning Source LLC
Chambersburg PA
CBHW031944090426
42739CB00006B/74